Deliverance, I

By

Lucretia Cargill

"A guide to the keys of Deliverance"

<u>PREFACE</u>

A spiritual guide designed for all individuals who need clarification on how God can and will deliver them out of troubling situations.

DELIVERANCE, Is My Testimony

By: Lucretia Cargill

Cover Designed by Lucretia Cargill

Cover Picture: Photo bucket

Editor: Lucretia Cargill

©2019 Lucretia Cargill

ISBN: 978-1975998721

ACKNOWLEDGEMENTS

First and foremost, I would like to give thanks and acknowledge God, my Lord and personal Saviour for using and giving me the wisdom and knowledge to write this book to inspire, encourage, and empower individuals who need a sense of direction to gain clarity, wisdom, and understanding on how God can deliver each of you out of troubling situations. I can do all things through Christ Jesus that strengthens me! God is *GOOD* and *AWESOME*! The works of the Lord is very powerful and should be treated and understood in a deserving manner. I had to learn that with God, nothing is impossible! I would also like to acknowledge my mother Mary B. Shaw for inspiring me in every step of my course in writing. Her instructions have kept me on the path to become successful and influential to others. My motivation is my children who have proven my ability to pursue my goals. I would like to thank all of you who have gotten a copy of this book to gain clarity on how God can deliver us out of any situation we face in our lives. And, most of all, on how to endure during the process. I pray that we all gain the wisdom and knowledge on how God can deliver us out of our troubles. God continues to forever reign in and throughout my life. With God, all things are possible (Matthew

19:26). I just can't thank God enough for using me to do His divine will.

Thank you all for the support and God bless!

<u>DEDICATIONS</u>

This book is dedicated to my family, my children, my church family, and all individuals who have the desire to want to know how to become free from troubling situations and trials in their lives when faced with adversities. God is a *Deliverer*! The key word to being delivered is that you have to WANT to be delivered! A lot of times, we as individuals are afraid to let God deliver us from our situations because we may think of what others may say. In this guide, you will obtain wisdom and knowledge on deliverance how I and others was delivered from troubling situations. I pray that this book will give each of you insight on how you can relinquish control over your life when you are faced with overwhelming obstacles and adversities. I thank God for giving me insight, a sense of direction, and inspiration to continue to stay the course and focus on my writing to glorify Him. I speak blessings upon everyone who read this book. God bless!

Table of Contents

<u>INTRODUCTION</u>

Are you struggling with sexual sin, drugs, adultery, demonic activity, alcohol, lack, sickness, etc.? Just to name a few. Well, I have struggled with some of those same issues and still struggling today with other issues. No one is exempt from troubling situations. But, I know a Saviour who can help you through those rough patches in your life and His name is Jesus. God is a *DELIVERER*! He's Almighty, the Alpha the Omega, the Beginning and the End, the First and the Last, the Head and not the Tail. He is everything we stand in need of. He knows our struggles and our pain. Look back over your life and see where God has brought you from. If you have ever been in a situation and then suddenly without a shadow of a doubt you've made it out or the situation got better. You didn't do it yourself, God made a way for you. Sometimes, we think that we are the ones who get ourselves out of a situation, but it is God who gives us the strength to endure the situations we face. He allows us to go through trying times, whereas, there is a purpose for our pain so we can draw a more personal relationship with Him. God wants us to trust Him even when we are going through our storms. When you are willing to make a change in your life, you must let God move on your behalf. I've seen people continue to struggle and live an unholy life that is displeasing

Deliverance, Is My testimony

to God. *"Deliverance"* is defined as "a rescue from bondage or danger". Deliverance, in the Bible is the acts of God, whereby, He rescues His people from peril. In the Old Testament, deliverance is focused primarily on God's removal of those who are in the midst of trouble or danger. He rescues His people from their enemies (I Samuel 17:37; 2 Kings 20:6), and from the hand of the wicked (Psalm 7:2; 17:13; 18:16-19; 59:2). He preserves them from famine (Psalm 33:19), death (Psalm 22:19-21), and the grave (Psalm 56:13; 86:13; Hosea 13:14). The most striking example of deliverance is the exodus from Egypt. (Exodus 3:8; 6:6, 8:10). Here is God defined as the Deliverer of Israel who rescues His people, not because they deserve to be rescued, but as an expression of His mercy and love (Psalm 51:1; 71:2, 86:13). In the New Testament, God is always the subject and His people are always the object of deliverance. The descriptions of temporal deliverance in the Old Testament serve as symbolic representations of the spiritual deliverance from sin which is available only through Christ. He offers deliverance from mankind's greatest peril-sin, evil, death, and judgment. By God's power, believers are delivered from this present evil age (Galatians 1:4) and from the power of Satan's reign (Colossians 1:13). All aspects of deliverance are available only through the person and work of Jesus Christ, who was Himself delivered up for us (Romans 4:25) so that we would be delivered from eternal punishment for sin. Only Jesus rescues us from the "wrath to come" (I Thessalonians 1:10). Another aspect of deliverance concerns the temporal. While believers are delivered once and for all time from eternal punishment, we are also delivered from the trials of this life (2 Peter 2:9). Sometimes, that deliverance is God simply walking through the trials by our side, comforting and encouraging us through them as He uses them to mature us in faith. Paul assured the Corinthian believers that "no hath temptation has seized you except what is common to man. And God is faithful; He will not let you be tempted beyond what you can bear. But when you are tempted, He will also provide a way out so that you can stand up under it" (I Corinthians 10:13). In these cases, rescue is not immediate, but in due time, after patience has had its perfect work (James 1:2-4, 12). God makes the way of escape simultaneously in His perfect will and timing. Deliverance is often sought from evil spirits or the spirit of lust, jealousy, envious etc. It's important to understand that as believers, we already have the eternal victory over Satan and demons. But we can be delivered from their influence in our lives by using two weapons God has given us as part of our spiritual armor with which we battle "against the spiritual forces of evil in the heavenly realms" (Ephesians 6:12-17). The believer defends himself with the shield of faith and uses the offensive weapon of the word of God. Against these two, no spirit can prevail. By holding up the shield of faith we can extinguish the flaming spiritual arrows they send against us of lust, doubt, guilt, jealousy, evil speech and all manner of temptations with the sword of the spirit, which is the word of God. We overcome the evil one by proving his temptations to be lies because he is the father of lies (John 8:44). John second letter commends the young Christians whose spiritual strength came from the Word of God living in them. By the offensive weapon of the truth, we overcome the evil one. (I John 2:14). You will know your deliverance. You will feel it. In the meantime, do something for God to deliver you out of your situation. God will deliver!! I'm concerned about serving God now, not what I'm going through. Despite every situation and trial you're facing, God will deliver. God is the infinite God. Deliverance from sin, rescue from trials, and escape from the influence of the world in the control of the evil one come only through Christ, the son of God who has come and has given us understanding, so that we may know Him and His truth. And we are in

Him who is true-even in His Son Jesus Christ. He is "true God and eternal life" (I John 5:19-20). When God sets you free, you will be walking in a different direction of life. In this book, you will gain clarity on how being delivered from your situations will not only open your eyes but also show you that God is in control of every situation. If you have faith and patience to wait on God, then you will reap the harvest if you faint not. Let Got DELIVER you!!!

CHAPTER 1

GOD'S PERFECT TIMING

While we were yet sinners, Christ died for us" (Romans 5:8). Even though we are undeserving, God died for the ungodly. He walked this earth as man to save the lost and the sick. God had performed many miracles back then and He is still performing miracles now. In the Old Testament, there are a lot of miracles that God performed. Have you ever faced impossible situations? Have you ever experienced that you needed deliverance but you were convinced that you could not help yourself? It was as if you faced a brick wall. No friends could help you, no relatives could deliver you. Even your wife or your husband could not help you. You were totally unable to deliver yourself. This reality can be deeply experienced in our lives. There can be situations in our lives that are most perplexing. For instance, there is a child who does not want to obey and is bent on destroying himself. There may be a financial crisis that you cannot avoid or a tragic accident that causes deep grief. There may be a parent, who is mentally ill and cannot be reached by reasoning, or you may suddenly become very ill and there is no cure for your illness. Death may be staring you in the face. We could continue with many more impossible situations that we have no understanding or control over but God is still in control of everything we face in life and life's circumstances. There can be impossible situations in spiritual life. God's Spirit convicts us and shows us that we are lost and without Christ. You realize that you need a mighty work of God's saving grace in your life. You see the power of indwelling sin, but are unable to curb it. You try to witness for Christ, but your words seem to fall on deaf ears. These are all impossible situations that are beyond our own power to solve. You realize you are completely helpless. There is only One who can help. That is the Lord himself. He has all authority and all power in heaven and on earth. He is mighty to save us because He is the Triune; God the Father, Son, and Holy Spirit. This reality gives light in the darkest situations. This awareness gives hope in the most hopeless situations. When you cannot help yourself anymore and no human being can deliver you, when all your ways are fenced in and you see no hope, there is still God. In Matthew 19, the disciples were also struck by the impossibility of being saved from man's side. But then we read in verse 26, but Jesus beheld them, and said unto them, *"With men this is impossible; but with God all things are possible."* We find the same thing in Mark 10:27. When the angel Gabriel informs Mary of the miraculous birth of the Messiah, he says, For with God nothing shall be impossible. (Luke 1:37). The Lord always work by ways and means that seem impossible. Just think of the patriarch Abraham who had to leave Ur of the Chaldeans and move to a far-away country. It was the most dangerous thing to do. Warlords and bandits were ready to kill him and steal his flocks. But Abraham went in faith, knowing that what is impossible with men is possible with God. Later, Abraham experienced the blow that his wife, Sarah, could not conceive a child. Abraham had to wait. Although, Sarah was far beyond the age of childbearing, God worked the impossible and she conceived and gave birth to a child. There were also Isaac and Rebekah. They needed a child to continue the covenant line of promise. Humanly speaking, this looked impossible. If they did not receive a child from the Lord they could not be saved. The Saviour had to come through the conception of a child and they knew it. They knew they must receive a child and they themselves were unable to bring this about. They faced impossibility. The reality of our impossibilities compared to God's almighty power, is continually underscored in scripture. The Lord always works along impossible ways. The existence of the church in this hostile world is an utter impossibility.

Deliverance, Is My testimony

How can the church continue to exist? How did it ever come into existence? There were just a few men from Galilee who were sent to preach a new doctrine. Could that be the beginning of the church? There is a crucified Saviour, but how can He save lost sinners? When He died the disciples thought everything was lost. They thought they could not go on. But the Lord gives a glorious outcome and showed His disciples that He conquers death by His own death. Later, when the Lord sends the disciples out to preach, it seems impossible to expect they can ever establish a church. From their side it is impossible. They will be killed instead! How was the church ever established? Matthew 16:18 states, *"And I say also unto thee, That thou art Peter, and upon this rock I will build my church; and the gates of hell shall not prevail against it"*. From man's side it is impossible. But again, Luke 18:27 states, *"The things which are impossible with men are possible with God."* The Lord worked along with the disciples and the Holy Spirit and blessed their preaching. The church was planted by God's irresistible power. How can the church survive in the hostile environment of severe persecutions? The answer, again, lies not in man, but in God. It is because the Lord Jesus said, *"And I give unto them eternal life; and they shall never perish, neither shall any man pluck them out of my hand* (John 10:28). God himself does what we cannot do. That has always been the secret of God's people. The spiritual birth of every one of them is impossibility. They are all dead in sins and trespasses, lost and unwilling to seek the Lord. They are all on the way to perdition and feel no conviction and have no concern. But the Lord did the impossible! Unwilling children are changed into people of God! Spiritual life is granted. A church is planted; it grows and exists wherever it pleases the Lord to plant His church. Despite overwhelming opposition, His church will continue to exist. In every generation, there will be those who will fear and love the Lord. That is His work. This is also experienced in our personal life. God works in spite of our impossibilities. There may be many perplexing questions, such as: How can I ever be righteous before God? How can I ever be converted? My heart is so hard, my heart is so cold and my heart is so unwilling. I cannot love Him as I should. All these observations are true. No good thing will ever come forth from sinful man, but our fruit and our spiritual life are found in Christ. It comes from Him! God works a glorious work and He saves to the uttermost. He enters sinners' hearts, changes and renews them. The blessed reality is that God grants deliverance. When you see only impossibilities in your life and all your ways are hedged up, there is still a God in heaven who can save to the uttermost. He hears the needy when they cry. He saves their souls from the greatest need. This can be a material or a spiritual need. When your sins accuse you and you see the need of the Lord Jesus in your heart, trust in Him. Call upon Him with expectation. He will not refuse you. You may lean on the Lord and put your hope in Him. Those who call upon the name of the Lord shall be saved. In spite of all their impossibilities, the Lord can give a full deliverance. Those who wait upon the Lord shall not be put to shame. In our daily lives, the Lord may lead us into impossible situations to show us His great power to deliver us from every need. The way to receive this deliverance is by prayer. The Lord Jesus has taught us in the parable of the unjust judge and the importunate widow that we should pray continually and we should not give up. At times, the Lord withholds the fulfilment for a while. In His wisdom, He does not always answer immediately. But deliverance comes at exactly the right time. It never comes too soon or too early. The Lord can bear with us for long and can seem to wait a long time before giving full deliverance to His people (Luke 18:7). There are many verses in scripture that call us to persevere in prayer. We are to knock because we are promised that it shall be opened unto us. We are to seek and promised that we shall find. By struggling in prayer, we may be encouraged by the rich promises of God. God's promises are lights shining in the darkness of afflictions. Commenting on Genesis 25:21, God shows that He never turns a deaf ear to the wishes of His faithful people, although He may long defer the answer. I am challenging you while you are on this journey to wait for your deliverance from God. God is the only one who can deliver us out of all of our troubles. There were plenty of times in my life that God had showed up right on time. It was when I least expected. Have you ever prayed for something and maybe a year or two later you see yourself out of the situation….Yesss…nobody but God! Everything has a season and perfect timing. We try to rush God to bring us out of our troubling situations but God can see everything up there. He knows when the perfect time for us to be delivered. I have been praying and praying for deliverance and I know my time is coming. It's all about being patient. Remember a delay, is not a denial!!!

CHAPTER 2

LIFE AND FAVOR

Due to different medical conditions, I've had in the past; I was in pain almost every day. Sometimes it was unbearable and other times it was manageable. The question that plagued my mind at times was why? Why can't I live a normal life pain free and not have my life interrupted daily by the conditions? What did I do to deserve this? After a careful observation of my life, to make sure I'm in right standing with God and others, I realized that it was because I decided at the age of 13 years old to give my life to Christ. When I finally realized that I needed to make a change in my life over 3 years ago, was when I fully surrendered my life to Christ withholding nothing asking God to increase the Holy Spirit within me and to use me for His glory. As Christ gave up His life on Calvary over 2000 years ago, I did the same that night I cried out to Him and received His precious gift of the Holy Spirit. During my pain, there were four things I had to realize that: **I am not my own:** *Or do you not know that your body is a temple of the Holy Spirit who is in you, whom you have from God, and that you are not your own? For you have been bought with a price: therefore, glorify God in your body. – I Corinthians*

6:19-20. The Christian life is a life of sacrifice. With Christ being our example, He sacrificed His life at a young age so we could be saved. It's only fitting for us to do the same for Him realizing He gave the ultimate sacrifice for us. When I pray, I specifically ask the Lord for His will to be done in my life. I am surrendering my will (my wants, my plans and my desire) for His will for my life. I'm relinquishing my rights for God to have His will and His way in my life. **God's way is not my way:** *For My thoughts are not your thoughts, nor are your ways my ways," declares the Lord – Isaiah 55:8.* Often, we want to put God in a box, the way we think things should be done but God is letting us know that He doesn't think the way we think. God desires to do exceedingly abundantly above all we can ask or think in our lives. We can't even comprehend the things God has in store for us. Sometimes when we see things for what they are, we get discouraged. But when we look at it through faith in God's word, we can see things the way God sees it. We may not be able to physically see it but we can spiritually visualize it through faith. I may not be able to see my healing now but I know God said in his word, "by His stripes I am healed." **Don't try to understand:** *Trust in the Lord with all your heart and do not lean on your own understanding. In all your ways* *acknowledge Him; And He will make your paths straight. – Proverbs 3:5-6.* One of my problems when going through was trying to understand why I am going through. But God reminds me in His word, to trust Him. Once I realized that it's not my job to understand but to just trust God, things begin to get better. I stopped stressing trying to figure it out and began trusting God to work it out. **Anytime is a good time to rejoice:** *For I consider that the sufferings of this present time are not worthy to be compared with the glory that is to be revealed to us. – Romans 8:18.* Why would someone rejoice while they are going through hard times? Because you are simply going "through" this is not your final destination. You just claimed healing on your body and deliverance from your current circumstances. Although, you may not see it physically but you can see it through faith so *Praise God*! You may be suffering now but what you are going through now will not compare to what's to come. The best is yet to come! God knows what you are going through and He cares. He just needs you to trust Him and have faith that in His perfect timing He will deliver. What you are currently going through is not only designed and crafted by God to make you stronger but it's to encourage others that will be blessed through your testimony. That's why it's vital not to give up or to give in but to hold on because someone's future is in your hands. As believers, we've all been there or will be there. We may earnestly seek God, but in return only sense His silence. And this silence can be difficult, frustrating, and even excruciating. The Bible tells the story of a man named Job, who was well acquainted with pain and suffering. In his pain and suffering, he cried out to God. He asked for answers. And he kept asking. His cries for God's help and relief were met only by God's deafening silence. As Christians, we are not always going to hear God's voice, but from Job we can learn a few practical things to do when God seems silent: **1. Examine your life:** Begin by asking yourself the question, Is there any unconfessed sin in my life? Make sure nothing is blocking you from being able to hear God's voice. Psalm 66:18 says, *"If I had not confessed the sin in my heart, my Lord would not have listened"* (New Living Translation). This requires looking deeper than the obvious. Ask yourself: Do I have wrong motives? Is there anything (or anyone) that I love more than God? As God brings things to mind, quickly ask for His forgiveness. And remember, there's no shame in repentance. This act of faith pleases God and restores our fellowship with Him. **2. Accept God's Sovereignty:** Recognize that God can be silent. There is no obligation for God to answer you, inform you or let you know anything. Like us, Job faced the choice of acknowledging —

or rejecting — the sovereignty of God. In response to his suffering and

loss, Job's wife suggests he curse God and die. Instead of following her

advice, Job chooses to let God be God. Job's response: *"Shall we indeed*

accept good from God and not accept adversity?" (Job 2:10) Accepting

God's sovereignty also means actively trusting God, realizing He is in

control and can be trusted. *"Though He slay me, I will hope in Him" (Job*

13:15). Nothing in Job's life, or ours, happens apart from God's

knowledge and plan. As we learn at the beginning of the Book of Job, God

was fully aware of all the things that were about to happen to Job. In fact,

He gave Satan permission to do these things in Job's life. At no point does

God release His control. **3. Listen to What God Is Saying**: Although,

God may seem silent regarding a specific request or petition, remember

that He is always in a constant state of communication with us. In fact, it

is possible that you already have an answer from God. The Bible is full of

specific answers about what is right and wrong as well as information

about God's character and His intention for us as His children and His

followers. So, don't forget to dig into God's Word — His written

communication to us — to find out what He has to say about the problems you're facing or the questions you're asking. As you read the Bible, ask God to speak to you through the Holy Spirit, who lives inside of you. Often, verses can have new significance considering current problems you are facing. **4. Recognize That Silence Can Be Intimate**: Silence can also be a sign of God's trust. To Job, God's silence could have been interpreted as neglect — that Jesus didn't care or didn't want to help him. This mirrors many of the emotions we feel when God doesn't immediately answer our cries for help. But in silence we are drawn into a new closeness to God and understanding of His power. When you are completely comfortable with a person, it is possible to sit in a room together and not utter a word. In love, silence can be a sign of intimacy. For Job, God's silence was also a result of the depth of their relationship. When Satan approached God, He said, "Have you considered My Servant Job?" (Job 1:8). In trust, God chose Job. **5. Keep Talking to God**: Just because God seems silent doesn't mean you should doubt Him or stop praying. God's silence isn't a license for us to turn our backs on Him. Instead, it's an invitation to press forward and seek Him even more diligently. For the 37 chapters of the Book of Job, God was silent. But in chapter 38, God answers — and questions Job. *"Where were you when I* *laid the foundation of the earth?" asks God. "Tell Me, if you have understanding" (Job 38:4).* God is in control and has been all along. He heard Job's cries for help. In trust, He waited for the perfect time to speak. Job was reminded that God answers prayer. We are a work in progress and it takes time to be delivered. We must go through the weeping, heartbreaks, disappointments, pain, and understanding where you come from etc., but it also takes gratitude to acknowledge and realize where God has brought you from. But when you are converted and delivered, you must strengthen your brother and your sister. Growing up and going through different life situations has opened my eyes to everything and everyone around me. I can remember at the age of 17, I started smoking, partying, drinking, and staying out late, hanging with the wrong friends. My mom would always come looking for me. Every time I used to ask my mom to let me go somewhere she told me "NO", I still went anyway. We all know the saying, *"A hard head carries a soft behind". Also, A disobedient child will not live their days out"* Well, of course growing up as a teenager and wanting to do things of the world and my way, I did what I wanted to do basically. Well, even though I did those things, I was a smart kid. I made straight A's throughout the school years. I graduated from High School with honors and college with a Bachelor's Degree in Business Administration at the top of my class with a 3.9. GPA. FAVOR!! In my mid 20's, the partying got heavy, the smoking, and the drinking. I used to club on Thursday, Friday, and Saturday. And then started going on Wednesday if it was something going on. It got to the point where I strayed away from the Church for a while. Of course, hanging out in the streets put a damper on my spirit. At that time, I just wanted to enjoy life, I thought and didn't care about what no one thought because I took care of myself. When I had my first child, that didn't slow me down, I was still in the world doing worldly things. After I had my second child it was the same thing. Things that I know I wasn't supposed to be doing, I was doing it and I knew in my heart that God was not pleased. God is longsuffering and He gives us time to get it right. If it wasn't for His grace and mercy, I don't know where I would be right now. In short, after I really got tired of living a repetitive lifestyle and my kids started getting older; I finally built up the nerve to talk to God. I started going back to Church, but I knew change did not come over night. I was feeling weary and downtrodden and no one physically could help me. I realized I had to make that first step so God could move in my life. So, as I gradually continued to go to Church I found myself every Sunday repenting. I would be in the club on Saturday and on Sunday I'm in Church repenting and taking the Lord's Supper in vain. I knew God was not pleased with my YO-YO Christianity life I was trying to live. As I grew closer and closer unto the Lord, I started seeing things differently. As I surrendered everything to God, He stripped every desire I had. We have to be sincere when we go to God. I asked God specifically to take the taste out of my mouth to stop smoking and I didn't know how He was going to do it because I couldn't do it on my own. One night I was lying in bed and my sinuses was draining. It felt like something was in my throat and I was short on breath and my throat was rattling. I just felt so bad. But my instinct instructed me to go the emergency room. "Always follow your first mind". As I got to the emergency room and went to the back, the doctor came in and ran some tests and he asked, "Do you smoke"? I couldn't speak so I just looked up at him and nodded my head. The doctor said these EXACT words to me, "STOP SMOKING"! Okay, Lord, I knew then that you were trying to tell me something. He told me I had a case of bronchitis in which I never had before. After, I left the emergency and was treated; I never touched a cigarette again!!! Glory to God! I believe if I hadn't of obeyed the voice of

Deliverance, Is My testimony

God, I probably wouldn't be here writing my testimony today. I have been smoke free for 6 years now! Alongside the smoking, a few months later I stopped drinking, then I gradually stopped going to the club. Everything I prayed for was coming to past. I came to conclusion that God had a plan for me the reason He has kept me this long time. I just had to figure out what it was. In your life, whatever you are facing or struggling, God will deliver you, but it takes patience. Deliverance comes from the Lord. Almost everyone needs one form of deliverance or the other, because there is hardly anyone without a problem. Is there any problem you have been trying to solve and has remained unsolved in spite of using all human comprehension, connection, and reasoning? Any issue that has been afflicting you and you want to be freed from it? Anything that has been giving you anxiety, worries, nightmares, and tears? Is it marital problems, drug addiction, sicknesses and diseases, financial lack, satanic oppression, open or secret sins, job loss, or bareness? The good news today is that God is the Deliverer. He is the sovereign Lord and Ultimate power belongs to Him. Because He is the Creator, He can recreate and remold all things to serve His purpose. He is ready and willing to set you free today if only you believe in Him, trust in Him, and cry to Him. The classic story of the deliverance of Shadrach, Meshach, and Abednego from the burning furnace through divine intervention and also of Daniel from the Lion's den best indicates the fact that deliverance comes from God. The story of Shadrach, Meshach and Abednego as told in Daniel chapter 3 of the Holy Bible shows these three individuals who were Servants of the Lord, who were thrown into a fiery furnace because they refused to indulge in Idolatry by bowing down to a ninety feet high and nine feet golden image as commanded by King Nebuchadnezzar of Ancient Babylon: "*Whoever does not fall down and worship will immediately be thrown into a blazing furnace.*" Nebuchadnezzar had decreed. Daniel 3:16-18 states: "*Shadrach, Meshach and Abednego replied to the king, "O Nebuchadnezzar, we do not need to defend ourselves before you in this matter. If we are thrown into the blazing furnace, the God we serve is able to save us from it, and he will rescue us from your hand, O king. But even if he does not, we want you to know, O king that we will not serve your gods or worship the image of gold you have set up".* They were eventually thrown into the fiery furnace but came out unhurt because the God in whom they trusted sent His angel to deliver them. This is a miracle human wisdom cannot explain Daniel a servant of God was also thrown into a Lion's den because he was adamant in worshipping the Lord God, the Creator, instead of an earthly King as decreed by Darius King of ancient Medes. Daniel 6:16-17 *"So the king gave the order, and they brought Daniel and threw him into the lions' den. The king said to Daniel, "May your God, whom you serve continually, rescue you! "A stone was brought and placed over the mouth of the den, and the king sealed it with his own signet ring and with the rings of his nobles, so that Daniel's situation might not be changed"* In proving that He is the Deliverer of all those that earnestly seek His name and trust in Him, God miraculously rescued His servant Daniel from the Lion's den- Daniel 6:21: *"Daniel answered, "O king, live forever! My God sent his angel and he shut the mouths of the lions.* The God that delivered Shadrach, Meshach, and Abednego from the fiery furnace and Daniel from the Lion's den is still able to deliver us from any afflictions or problems in our lives. There are, however, several conditions for your deliverance. As shown in the stories above, you have to believe in God, trust in Him and serve Him continually. It goes without saying that if you are not a born again Christian who has totally surrendered his life to Jesus Christ, God, the Deliverer; He cannot intervene in your case. Do you need to be delivered TODAY? The only person that can deliver you is God, the

Creator and Supreme Being. There is no hope in any other name, religions of the world or any forms of satanic powers like astrology, occultism, witchcraft or idolatry. Cry to the true living God today, and He will deliver you from the problems of life. The only condition of your deliverance is accepting the Lord God as your Saviour, Jesus Christ. *"For God so loved the world that He gave His only begotten Son, that whoever believes in Him should not perish but have everlasting life."* -John 3:16. Romans 10:13: *For "whoever calls on the name of the Lord shall be saved".* Romans 10:9: *"that if you confess with your mouth the Lord Jesus and believe in your heart that God has raised Him from the dead, you will be saved."* Do you want to be reconciled with God, through Jesus the Lord and Saviour? Then say this simple prayer: *Father, in the name of Jesus Christ. I acknowledge that I am a sinner and have fallen short of your glory. I genuinely repent from all my sins and pledge to go and sin no more. I accept your plan to reconcile mankind to you through Jesus Christ, who you sent in your name. I believe Jesus Christ is the Messiah, and died on the Cross to pay the penalty for my sins and redeem me. I accept Jesus as my Lord and personal Saviour. I pray that His blood washes my sins away. I invite the Holy Spirit to rule my life. I am born*

Deliverance, Is My testimony

again in Jesus name. Amen I will continue to let God reign in and throughout my life. I surrender Lord!

CHAPTER 3

KEYS TO DELIVERANCE

There are different areas that we need to be delivered from. Let's go in depth with some areas that we need deliverance: <u>We need deliverance from the guilt and penalty of sin</u>: the illustration of this is in Luke 18:9-14, and the promise is in Acts 13:38-39. Luke's passage records our Lord's parable of two men, a Pharisee and a publican. There are types of men and women today. Both were sinners and both were guilty before God (Romans 3:23). The Pharisee, however, thought that God would accept him because of his supposed goodness (verses 9-12). There is absolutely no hope of deliverance from sin's penalty on the grounds of anything good in ourselves (Romans 3:20; Ephesians 2:8-10; Titus 3:5). The only way to be delivered from the penalty of sin is to look to Jesus and trust in His work on the cross. This is indicated in the publican's prayer (Luke 18:13). He prayed, *"God, have mercy on me, a sinner"*. What was the result? Verse 14 tells us. <u>We need deliverance from the power of evil</u>: the illustration of this is in Romans 7:18-25, and the promise is in Romans 6:14. What a tremendous struggle is described in the verses in Romans 7! Here is a Christian, conscious of the battle which is going on between his old nature and his new nature, having received his new nature through faith in Christ. Notice the agonizing cry in verse 24. How greatly this man needed deliverance, and how he longed to be set free from spiritual and moral bondage! Verse 25 tells us he was set free. We need deliverance from sudden temptation: the illustration of this is in Genesis 39:1-23, and the promise is in 1 Corinthians 10:13.We know what it's like to be faced with sudden temptation, though possibly not the kind that threatened Joseph. Study Genesis 39 carefully, and notice the terrible temptation which came to him and the courageous way he overcame (verses 7-12); then notice how the whole situation was aggravated (verses 14-20); and finally, notice the word *"but"* in verse 21, and the words that follow on into verse 23. So there is deliverance for the child of God in times of sudden temptation, and here is the promise for you. We need deliverance from gripping fear: the illustration of this is in Psalm 34:4 and the promise is in Proverbs 1:33. It has been suggested that those whose testimonies are recorded in the early part of Psalm 34 were some of David's men who were with him in the cave of Adullam. One of these gives a testimony which will help us. He says, *"I sought the Lord, and he answered me; he delivered me from all my fears."* (Psalm 34:4) So, he was gripped by fear.

What did he do? He brought his fears to the Lord and told Him of his need of deliverance and what happened? He tells us that he was delivered from all his fears and it is important to notice the word "all" and if you look up Proverbs 1:33, you will see the Lord's promise to us about His willingness to free us from fear and to give us peace through faith in Him. His desire for us is illustrated in Mark 4:39. We need deliverance from depression and loneliness: the illustration of this is in 1 Kings 19:1-15, and the promise is in Isaiah 41:10.In 1 Kings chapters 17, 18 and 19 we see Elijah's faith shining out at the brook Cherish and in the widow's house at Zarephath. On Mount Carmel we see it again, and his challenge to the powers of darkness. He stood up to Ahab, Jezebel and the prophets of Baal what victory! – And then, suddenly, poor Elijah, tired and exhausted, fled for his life (1 Kings 19:3-4). He felt dejected, fearful and depressed and he even prayed to die! He suffered a spiritual collapse, but God came to his help and delivered him. We need deliverance from difficult situations: the illustration of this is in Daniel 6:14-23, and the promise are in Psalm 34:7. Daniel was brought before the officials in Babylon for his fidelity to God, as a result of which he was thrown to the lions (Daniel 6:16-17). When he was safely sealed in the lions' den, King Darius was also doing something (verses 18-22). In verse 22 we read of his miraculous deliverance, and in verses 26-27 of the king's decree which ascribed glory to God who had delivered His servant Daniel. <u>We need deliverance from resentment and bitterness:</u> the illustration of this is in Acts 7:54-60, and the promise is in Psalm 50:15.Read about Stephen and his defense at the beginning of Acts chapter 7. Study verses 54-60, and notice his amazing calm and submission, and the fine testimony he gave, even under provocation. We can easily become bitter and resentful when trouble comes and we question God's dealings with us, but as Stephen was being stoned he glorified God. *GOD HAS GIVEN US POWER OVER THE ENEMY. IF YOU BELIEVE CHRIST CAME TO SET THE CAPTIVES FREE, THEN DELIVERANCE IS FOR YOU.* If you are a believer, then Jesus has given you the authority to represent Him. Mark 16:17-18 tells us: *"These signs will follow those who believe: In My name they will cast out demons; they will speak with new tongues: they will take up serpents; and if they drink anything deadly, it will by no means hurt them; they will lay hands on the sick, and they will recover".* Every believer has the ability to cast out devils. A believer who does not cast out devils is like a person who carries around a gift card but never uses it. We come to Jesus in need of salvation and release from the grips of the evil one and his lifestyle. Once we are released, a sure sign of spiritual growth in Christ is the manifestation of the signs of the believers mentioned above. You cannot get around the ministry of casting out devils if you want to walk in the full Gospel. Unless you believe in deliverance, you are not fulfilling the entire purpose of Christ for your life as outlined in His Word. Jesus came to set the captives free. He could have sat in heaven and loosed fire on the devil's head, but He came down as a man, as an example to us that we can resist and attack demonic forces in victory. God gets no pleasure out of watching the devil attack and destroy His children. Jesus hijacked the devil and gave us the keys. Now He sits at the right hand of the Father and watches to see what we will do with them. The traditional way of living out our Christianity is to somehow just "make it" until Jesus comes back "in the sweet by and by." But God is rising up an apostolic generation with a different spirit. This generation has the spiritual balance to dig up the wells of their forefathers and draw from their inheritance. But they will not follow the traditions of men that were designed to keep people out of the Promised Land. Know who you are in Christ Jesus and who He is in you! Who you are in Him qualifies you for heaven and who He is in you authorizes you to do greater works than He did in the earth. The strategy

of God's kingdom is this: God's will has come to Earth. Jesus told Peter:

"'I will give you the keys of the kingdom of heaven, and whatever you bind

on earth will be bound in heaven, and whatever you loose on earth will be

loosed in heaven"(Matthew 16:19).You are the devil's worst nightmare!

Once you grasp the revelation that you were born to terrorize darkness,

you will stop running from situations that are designed to take you out of

the will of God. Pray that God will give you a burden for setting people

free. Once your heart becomes heavy from seeing the devil hold captive

the people with whom you have daily contact, you will have a hunger to

see souls not only delivered from sin but also set free from the demonic

control of Satan and his evil spirits. God has given us a revelation of the

believer's authority over hell. Binding and loosing is a high level of

spiritual warfare. In binding, we confront the enemy and forbid him to

operate. When we lose, we cause a breakthrough in the spiritual realm. We

pave the way through warfare prayer and the will of God is released (see

Matthew 6:10).You make a spiritual connection when you engage the

enemy in prayer. You actually come into agreement with heaven (see

Matthew 18:19). Then, the keys are given to us to shut up demonic activity, and that's when the breakthrough happens! How you pray has a lot to do with how effective you are on Earth. James told his church that they did not have what they were praying for because they were not praying the right prayers. *"You ask and do not receive, because you ask amiss, that you may spend it on your pleasures"* (James 4:3).If we are not praying prayers that are the will of God, then, we are praying prayers out of our own flesh. Fleshly prayers do not move the heart of God. They are futile. But a kingdom-minded person has an apostolic attitude and is not drawn to carnality. He or she is drawn, which causes the kingdom of God to come. In order to be effective deliverance workers, intercessors or ministers, we need to "practice what we preach." Paul made this point in 1 Corinthians 9:26-27: "I don't know about you, but I'm running hard for the finish line. I'm giving it everything I've got. No sloppy living for me! I'm staying alert and in top condition. I'm not going to get caught napping, telling everyone else all about it and then missing out myself (The Message). It is easy for most believers to recognize Satan as evil, but it seems to be difficult for some to see their flesh as evil. However, it is the season for the saints of God to get their houses in order. Accept the fact that your flesh has a mind of its own (see Romans 8:5-8). It must be sternly dealt with, or it will run the house. Getting deliverance is one thing; sustaining it is another. There are several spiritual keys to maintaining your deliverance: **<u>Key No. 1: Remain connected.</u>** First Peter 5:8 warns us that our adversary is seeking whom he may devour. One of his primary targets is a believer who does not have the proper spiritual connection or covering in two areas: *Leadership.* God gave gifts (the fivefold ministry) to the church for the maturity of the saints (see Ephesians. 2:20). Individual believers need to be touched by each of the fivefold ministries of the church--including the apostolic and prophetic ministries. *Fellowship.* God warns us not to forsake the assembling of ourselves together (see Hebrews. 10:24-25). Those who allow themselves to be separated from the flock will be devoured by the lion. In the days of Joshua, the Israelites were known as people of victory. They were famous for deliverance. But their challenge was dealing with the spoils of their victory. In Joshua's case, God commanded that they not take any of the enemy's goods (see Joshua. 6:18). The four lepers who sat at the gate of Samaria were to take of the goods, but hoarding them would cause them to lose their deliverance (see 2 Kings 7). When God has delivered you and you obtain victory in an area of your life, you must have an ear to hear the further instructions of the Lord. God takes you from one level to the next, but there are new devils on every level. When you get saved and delivered, you do not join a club membership, you enroll in the greatest army ever! God is taking His people from a "membership mentality" to a "warfare mentality" (see Judges. 3:1).**Key No. 3: Study the Word of God.** Second Timothy 2:15 says that if you study the Word of God, you will not be ashamed. It also says that studying the Word will give you the ability to rightfully divide the word of truth. The urgency of studying the Word is made clear in the story of Hymenaeus and Philetus (see 2 Timothy. 2:16-18). They made an error concerning the truth that caused them to lose their deliverance and to be turned over to Satan. Their sin was said to be blasphemy. According to 2 Timothy 2:16, vain babblings will increase and lead to more ungodliness. When you do not rightfully divide the truth, it will devour your deliverance. **Key No. 4: Break old ties and soul ties.** Second Corinthians 5:17 describes true deliverance. Old things are passed away, and, when people see us, all things in our lives appear new. Romans 12:2 say to be "transformed" into the image of Christ and not "conformed" to the image of the world. The image of the world represents what you've come out of. The image of Christ is what you are moving toward. The "new man" will not fit over the old man. Just like a floor that must be stripped and buffed before it is waxed, you must be stripped of every troubling sin or weight. Stay away from the thing from which you have been delivered (see Hebrews. 12:1).**Key No. 5: Guard your thought life.** You are only as delivered as you think you are (see Proverbs 23:7).My strongest bondages were cigarettes. After I was set free by the power of Jesus Christ, the devil would place images before me to make me think I was still bound by the addiction. He told me I was still a smoker. But I knew I was free. When Satan spoke, I heard him from afar because God's voice was so much louder. God said that we would know His voice and this would help us not to follow the enemy (see John 10:5).People think that when the devil speaks to them, something is wrong. But if he is speaking to you, you are doing something right. Take responsibility for your deliverance. Once you have submitted yourself to God, learn to resist the devil. If you do, he must flee! (See James 4:7.)The devil is not trying to talk you out of what you do not have. He is targeting you because you have something he wants. Guard your thought life from the enemy. He wants to confuse you and cause you to doubt your purpose in God. Any voice that does not speak the truth (the Word) is of the devil.

Deliverance, Is My testimony

So, be alert in this time. When the children of Israel were delivered from Egypt, their greatest challenge was coming out of a bondage mentality. When God sets us free, the enemy attempts to get us to remember the good things about our former bondage because he wants to make serving God seem harder. We must move forward! People who are stagnated spiritually have no prophetic insight. Go forth based on the Word of the Lord that has been given to you. The greatest aspect of deliverance is hope. It gives us a foundation for our faith. Your faith must stand trial. The Lord spoke to Moses and told him to tell the people to move forward (see Exodus. 14:15). They could not be concerned about the Red Sea in front of them. It always takes faith to move forward. Lot was delivered out of Sodom and commanded never to look back. When his wife looked back, she lost her deliverance (see Genesis. 19:27).Obstacles will attempt to make you doubt. Soul ties will make you want to look back. Always remember that Jesus is the Author and Finisher of our faith. He brought you out, and surely, He will take you in! The enemy tempted Jesus, and no matter how anointed you are, he will continue to tempt you also. But when temptation comes to steal your deliverance, you can make a statement that has helped me during the years: "Jesus, I love you more"! Truly loving

Deliverance, Is My testimony

God instills reverential fear. The fear of the Lord is a sure foundation. Deliverance is for everyone! And as God's agents on Earth, we have authority to defeat and destroy the enemy and his spirits whenever we encounter them. Weapons will form against us, but they will not prosper because we possess an arsenal on the inside of us that will annihilate darkness!

CHAPTER 4
REDEMPTION

Idly, sitting in Church one morning and the song leader started singing "I'm redeemed"! As that song registered in my mind, I started thinking to myself, "I too have been redeemed"! The Holy Spirit was certainly moving in the church while singing that song which brought tears to my eyes. Looking back over my life and all the trials and situations I faced, I never thought I would be where I am today. God can do the impossible and can make some changes in your life if you want it. *Redemption* means to free someone from bondage. It often involves the paying of a ransom, a price that makes redemption possible. The Israelites were redeemed from Egypt. We were redeemed from the power of sin and the curse of the Law (Galatians 3:13) through Jesus (Romans 3:24; Col. 1:14). We were bought with a price (1 Corinthians 6:20; 7:23). Originally, the payment of a price to secure the release of a prisoner of war, the word came to be used also of the release of a slave and sometimes of a person under sentence of death (Exodus. 21:28-30). Redemption always means the payment of a price to secure release. People who sin become slaves of sin (John 8:34); they cannot free themselves from that slavery. Christ's death on the cross was the payment of a ransom price (Mark 10:45) by which sinners were set free. Now that we are redeemed, we must live as free people (1 Corinthians 6:19-20; Galatians 5:1). I've learned that the Bible is a book of redemption. God wants us to communicate the story through His word. There are so many Bible stories about redemption that I love to read about. For example: The story of Noah, God warned of a coming judgment. This was going to be a world-wide punishment. Those who would repent of their sins and believe in the warning of Noah were welcome to board the ark before the flood waters began to fall. After 120 years of preaching, the only people who stepped onto the ark were Noah and his family. Though there was room for many more people in the ark, only eight souls were saved. Redemption was offered to all who would repent and believe (Genesis 6-8). There are so many life changing situations we have when we become redeemed. By God's grace, I have been redeemed. *In him we have redemption through his blood, the forgiveness of our trespasses, according to the riches of his grace,* Ephesians 1:7. We've all been there, feeling guilty for having sinned against God. Feeling tired of saying sorry to Him but committing the same sins or worse over again. We beat ourselves up and think of thoughts not according to the will of God. Then, the enemy attacks us by using our own thoughts to condemn us. As much as we don't want to, we will make mistakes. We will commit sins. We will break God's heart again and again. We will repent, then break His heart some more. That's the reality as long as we are human and living in our earthly bodies. No one is perfect. *For all have sinned and fall short of the glory of God* (Romans 3:23). But the awesome thing about God is that He forgives us if we repent wholeheartedly (and we should not use this as an excuse to willfully sin and disobey Him time and time again). The good news is... It's not too late for God to work wonders through you. He is not limited by anything at all – even our sins – in accomplishing His plans for us. Need proof? Let me tell you five Bible stories about 5 men of God who have committed unspeakable acts of evil and how God turned their lives around: David We all know David as the man who slayed the giant Goliath and the "man after God's own heart". On the other hand, in the book of 2 Samuel Chapter 11, we learn about how King David committed adultery with Bathsheba and how he had Uriah (Bathsheba's husband) killed. Paul Before he was called to be God's apostle, Saul of Tarsus was one of the great persecutors of Christians. He went from one house to another, dragging believers on their feet on the way to the prison. He was also present during the stoning of Stephen, who is believed to be the first Christian martyr. For these reasons, Paul called himself "chief of sinners". Moses Committed murder before God called him to lead the Israelites out of Egypt. This was illustrated to us in the book of Exodus chapter 2. He saw an Egyptian who was hitting his Hebrew brother, so he got even by killing him and hiding him in the sand and then he escaped. Jonah He was that guy who spent three days and three nights in the belly of a big fish because of his disobedience to God. God commanded Jonah to preach to Nineveh but instead of following God's direct order, he rode a ship to Tarshish so he can run from God (as if it were possible). Solomon The son of King David was famous for his wisdom and his riches. But he disobeyed God by allowing his 700 wives and 300 concubines lead him to worship idols. These five great men of God all have disobeyed God's laws. But then after further reading and study, we learn that they all repented and they were used mightily for God's glory. Does that mean we should continue sinning since we can repent anyways afterwards? As Apostle Paul stated in Romans 6:1, certainly not! When we sin, God is gracious enough to forgive us but our disobedience has consequences.

Deliverance, Is My testimony

What amazes me most is that even as we deal with the consequences of our sins, God is with us. He gives us the grace to move forward. It was even declared in Romans 8:28 *"that all things work together for good to those who love God, to those who are the called according to His purpose."* And lastly, unlike the 5 men above, we have Jesus Christ, the greatest gift we have received from our Heavenly Father. He bore the cross and suffered all the shame and condemnation for us. What more can we ask for? So, the next time the enemy reminds you of the sins you have committed, throw him this verse from Galatians 2:20 (which I firmly believe he's familiar with): *I have been crucified with Christ; it is no longer I who live, but Christ lives in me; and the life which I now live in the flesh I live by faith in the Son of God, who loved me and gave Himself for me.* We are imperfect people loved by a perfect God. Our Saviour and Lord Jesus Christ paid it all on the cross. People ask me, how did I get this way? Growing up as a child me and my sisters coming from the struggle has taught me how to be a survivor. We never had what other kids had. With a Christian background of my family, I was brought up in the Church but strayed away during the years. Listen, I have not always been this way or knew what I wanted to be in life, but I knew what type of woman I wanted to be. I could hear a calling, but I got distracted by so many other things. Throughout my life, I went through a lot of heartache, pain, disappointments, betrayal, physically and mentally abused, mistreated, used, and being broken. Even during the midst of my storms, I was still able to keep my head held high with a smile on my face. I always knew that God had a plan for my life, but didn't know what it was. The woman back then didn't know what she wanted out of life, but I knew in order for me to get there, I had to start walking in a different direction to get a different result. I learned to heal, forgive, and grow from my past that was haunting me daily. I learned to face my past head on and learned from it. I knew that my past did not define me. I knew that no matter what I faced, God was always there. And that He was still in control. A long the way I lost friends and family, but I have also gained. I once was blind but now I see. By the grace of God I am still here today. I am a woman clothed in strength. My mission is to inspire, uplift, empower, and encourage all countless individuals to start walking in a different direction to get a different result. I looked back over my life and saw where God has brought me from. He brought me from a mighty long way. We are to be a light of the world and I know that God is not through with me yet. I've been through the fire and didn't get burned! I'm in the soul saving and life changing business and God has lifted me up to a higher plane to help others get to where they need to be. Being able to inspire and encourage others bring joy to my soul. God gets the glory behind this! Everything you are going through in your lives, let God work it out. I have people telling me everywhere you are one strong woman. Listen, I didn't get here overnight. It took a lot of weeping and bad situations for me to get here. You have to go through to get through!!! My mom did what she could as a single mother raising 3 daughters with the help of my grandmother and great grandmother. My mother fought to do her best but hardships never missed us. I've learned in life that your struggles give you strength. I know what it feels like to be broken, confused, betrayed, and hated, etc. I thank God for allowing me to share my story and inspire each individual on a daily basis! I'm not perfect but I have a purpose! The same God, who brought me out, is the same God who will bring you out! Everyone deserves to live the life that God has ordained for us to live! God is no respector of persons. He loves and treats us all the same. So, I'm challenging each and every one of you on today to RECLAIM your DESTINY! We all have been redeemed by the grace of God. Look back over your life and see how far you have come throughout the years and how God has restored you. *"With God, all things are possible"*-Matthew 19:26

CHAPTER 5
GRACE AND MERCY

"Let us therefore come boldly unto the throne of grace, that we may obtain mercy, and find grace to help in time of need" (Hebrews 4:16).God's grace and mercy can be viewed as two sides of the same coin. Grace on one side gives us what we do not deserve. Mercy on the other does not give us what we do deserve. Grace, often defined as unmerited favor, is offered freely by God "through the redemption that is in Christ Jesus" (Romans 3:24). It is offered to us only through faith in Christ so that we may clearly understand that it is not obtainable by any adherence to the law. *"For the law was given by Moses, but grace and truth came by Jesus Christ"* (John 1:17).The law is holy, just, and good (Romans 7:12), but unfortunately it magnifies our sin and shows us how far we are from reaching the perfect standard of our holy and righteous Creator. Thankfully, God's amazing grace overpowers our magnified sin, as it "super abounds" above our transgressions. *"But where sin abounded, grace did much more abound"* (Romans 5:20).God is also rich in His mercy toward us (Ephesians 2:4), as He extends His loving compassion to us despite our sinful condition. Our salvation is rooted in God's mercy as

Deliverance, Is My testimony

He hath begotten us again unto a lively hope by the resurrection of Jesus Christ from the dead (1 Peter 1:3).Grace and mercy are glorious gifts from God that should take us to our knees in worship and adoration. We can bring absolutely nothing to God except a humble and thankful heart as we trust not in our works, but solely in the finished work of Jesus Christ at Calvary. *"Not by works of righteousness which we have done, but according to His mercy He saved us"* (Titus 3:5). Thank God that *"His mercy endureth forever"* (Psalm 136:26). The qualities of God's character by which He shows himself compassionate, accepting, and generous to sinful human beings, shielding them from His wrath, forgiving them, and bestowing on them His righteousness so that they can live and grow in faith and obedience. Grace and mercy are particularly expressed through God's covenant with His chosen people and through Jesus Christ atoning death on the cross. Mercy and grace are often confused. While the terms have similar meanings, grace and mercy are not the same. To summarize the difference: mercy is God not punishing us as our sins deserve, and grace is God blessing us despite the fact that we do not deserve it. Mercy is deliverance from judgment. Grace is extending kindness to the unworthy and showing mercy to us when we have fallen by God's grace from our own sins. According to the Bible, we have all sinned (Ecclesiastes 7:20; Romans 3:23; 1 John 1:8). As a result of that sin, we all deserve death (Romans 6:23) and eternal judgment in the lake of fire (Revelation 20:12-15). With that in mind, every day we live is an act of God's mercy. If God gave us all what we deserve, we would all be, right now, condemned for eternity. In Psalm 51:1-2, David cries out, *"Have mercy on me, O God, according to your unfailing love; according to your great compassion blot out my transgressions. Wash away all my iniquity and cleanse me from my sin."* A plea to God for mercy is asking Him to withhold the judgment we deserve and instead grant to us the forgiveness we in no way have earned God is faithful and just. We deserve nothing from God. God does not owe us anything. Anything good that we experience is a result of the grace of God (Ephesians 2:5). Grace is simply defined as unmerited favor. God favors, or gives us good things that we do not deserve and could never earn. Rescued from judgment by God's mercy, grace is anything and everything we receive beyond that mercy (Romans 3:24). Common grace refers to the sovereign grace which God bestows on all of mankind regardless of their spiritual standing before Him, while saving grace is that special dispensation of grace whereby God sovereignly bestows unmerited divine assistance upon His elect for their regeneration and sanctification will be earned through Christ. Mercy and grace are best illustrated in the salvation that is available through Jesus Christ. We deserve judgment, but if we receive Jesus Christ as Saviour, we receive mercy from God and we are delivered from judgment. Instead of judgment, we receive by grace salvation, forgiveness of sins, abundant life (John 10:10), and an eternity in Heaven, the most wonderful place imaginable (Revelation 21-22). Because of the mercy and grace of God, our response should be to fall on our knees in worship and thanksgiving. Hebrews 4:16 declares, "*Let us then approach the throne of grace with confidence, so that we may receive mercy and find grace to help us in our time of need.*" God has showed grace and mercy for me even when I couldn't see in the physical eye. There were so many times I was in situations where I could have been dead and gone, but God saw differently. I asked God to order my steps in His Word and He did just that. I wanted to give up so many times in life but God had a plan for me to keep going. God's grace is sufficient and His mercy endureth forever! Have God shown you grace and mercy in a situation that was life threatening? God is known to be a God of mercy and grace.

Understanding mercy is often difficult for people as we tend to be a generation of "I'll get him for that" and "I hope they get what they deserve." Many have developed a nature of harsh criticism and want others to get what they have coming to them and then some. God, however, is merciful to even the worst offenders, sinners, and law-breakers. This means that even though He knows of our guilt, He doesn't always issue the punishment we deserve. Simply, we are all sinners and do not meet the standards of righteousness that God intends for us to have. But, through His mercy and grace He provided a way for our sins to be forgiven through our acceptance of Christ Jesus—even though we don't deserve it. Coupled with grace (being given God's free gift of forgiveness though we've done nothing to deserve it), mercy is shown because He loves us and only asks that we accept His Son by faith. The God of mercy calls for the following in <u>Micah 6:8</u>: *He hath shewed thee, O man, what is good; and what doth the Lord require of thee, but to do justly, and to love mercy, and to walk humbly with thy God?* These are words to all of mankind. Mercy is offered to you and me alike. He has shown us what is good and answers what is required of us. Micah asks God in <u>Micah 7:18</u>, "*Who is God like unto thee that pardoneth iniquity and passeth by the transgression of the remnant of his heritage"*? You do not stay angry forever but delight to show mercy." This passage shows that God enjoys being merciful and is still showing mercy today. One example of God's mercy today is the remarkable story of a woman called Jeanette. Her grandmother, Carla, tried to urge Jeanette to go into drug rehab without much success. Carla prayed to God, asking for His intervention with Jeanette. Carla was reminded by the words from God, "Be still, and know that I am GOD"! I can take that drug away from your granddaughter, squash it and it will not return." Carla said she prayed for Jesus to come into their broken family and heal her granddaughter. Jeanette is now drug free and enjoying a blessed relationship with her family. Carla stands on Luke 1:50, *"His mercy extends to those who fear [revere] him, from generation to generation."* There are many references about God's mercy throughout the Bible. For instance, in Genesis 37 through 45 we find the story of Joseph, son of Jacob. God's mercy toward Joseph's brothers for their betrayal is certainly evident in this story. Other illustrations are found throughout the prayers of King David in the Psalms. God's mercy is endless and found throughout the ages to the present. Paul gives a good picture of this in Ephesians 2:1-10. "As for you, you were dead in your transgressions and sins, in which you used to live when you followed the ways of this world and of the ruler of the kingdom of the air, the spirit who is now at work in those who are disobedient. All of us also lived among them at one time, gratifying the cravings of our sinful nature and following its desires and thoughts. Like the rest, we were by nature objects of wrath. But because of his great love for us, God, who is rich in mercy, made us alive with Christ even when we were dead in transgressions—it is by grace we are saved. And God raised us up with Christ and seated us with Him in the heavenly realms in Christ Jesus, in order that in the coming ages He might show the incomparable riches of His grace, expressed in His kindness to us in Christ Jesus. For it is by grace you have been saved, through faith—and this not from yourselves, it is the gift of God—not by works, so that no one can boast. For we are God's workmanship, created in Christ Jesus to do good works, which God prepared in advance for us to do." Mercy is a part of God's nature. How important is mercy to us? And where does grace fit into the picture? Mercy is commonly defined as forbearance or kindness. In particular, mercy usually involves kindness shown at a time when a severe penalty is expected. Mercy is one of God's traits, shown often toward mankind, as shown by this statement from Moses to the children of Israel: *"When you are in distress, and all these things come upon you in the latter days, when you turn to the LORD your God and obey His voice (for the LORD your God is a merciful God), He will not forsake you nor destroy you, nor forget the covenant of your fathers which He swore to them"* (Deuteronomy 4:30-31).Mercy is often tied to the concept of forgiveness. For instance, if you forgive someone who has wronged or hurt you, that would be an act of mercy. The book of Numbers illustrates this with the account of the children of Israel when they sent spies to the Promised Land. Ten of the 12 spies brought back a negative report about the land. The Israelites reacted with mourning and complaining and wanted to choose a new leader to take them back to Egypt, in spite of the many great miracles God had performed for them. This rebellion greatly angered God, and when He was ready to destroy the people, Moses intervened and appealed to God's mercy: "And now, I pray, let the power of my Lord be great, just as you have spoken, saying, 'The Lord is longsuffering and abundant in mercy, forgiving iniquity and transgression; but He by no means clears the guilty. …' Pardon the iniquity of this people, I pray, according to the greatness of Your mercy, just as You have forgiven this people, from Egypt until now"(Numbers 14:17-19).God responded, *"I have pardoned, according to your word"* (verse 20).While the Bible often talks about mercy in reference to sins and transgressions, that isn't always the case. At times, we can have mercy (or receive it) in situations of trial or discomfort, as shown in this passage in Proverbs: *"He who despises his neighbor sins; but he who has mercy on the poor, happy is he"* (Proverbs 14:21).All of these passages refer to an act of kindness or forgiveness toward someone who is in need of it. Although, mercy is certainly an aspect of God's grace, grace is a broader, more extensive concept than mercy. Grace comes from the Greek word *charis*, which has multiple meanings, including gift, favor and kindness. It refers to the unearned favor of God that is extended to us to pardon our sins upon repentance and to enable us to have a healthy, happy relationship with our Creator. Our sins being forgiven by God's grace leads to salvation (Titus 2:11). "Of this salvation the prophets have inquired and searched carefully, who prophesied of the grace that would come to you, searching what, or what manner of time, the Spirit of Christ who was in them was indicating when He testified beforehand the sufferings of Christ and the glories that would follow" (1 Peter 1:10-11).Grace is often mentioned in the context of guilt.

Deliverance, Is My testimony

We have all sinned, and the price for those sins is death. That penalty was paid for by the sacrifice of Jesus Christ. *"For all have sinned and fall short of the glory of God, being justified freely by His grace through the redemption that is in Christ Jesus"* (Romans 3:23-24). Grace involves the unmerited pardon of our sins, and that pardon was made possible by Christ death. God's grace will be made available to *all* mankind! When the apostles gathered in a conference in Jerusalem and debated how Gentiles as well as Israelites could receive salvation, Peter made the following statement: *"But we believe that through the grace of the Lord Jesus Christ we shall be saved in the same manner as they"* (Acts 15:11). The apostles went on to listen to accounts of how God had worked with the gentiles— pardoning their sins and giving them the Holy Spirit. Grace is what allows us to be cleansed of our sins and to be reconciled to our Creator: *"To the praise of the glory of His grace, by which He made us accepted in the Beloved. In Him we have redemption through His blood, the forgiveness of sins, according to the riches of His grace"* (Ephesians 1:6-7). Now consider this passage from the apostle Paul: "And I thank Christ Jesus our Lord who has enabled me, because He counted me faithful, putting me into the ministry, although I was formerly a blasphemer, a persecutor, and

Lucretia Cargill

an insolent man but I obtained mercy because I did it ignorantly in unbelief. And the grace of our Lord was exceedingly abundant, with faith and love which are in Christ Jesus" (1 Timothy 1:12-14). Here, we clearly see that the meaning of grace is broader than that of mercy. Paul had reason to expect punishment or harsh treatment because of his zealous persecutions of the early Christians. Instead, he received unexpected benevolence and forgiveness. He himself was called to be a Christian and a minister of the truth! That mercy, however, did not forgive his sins and justify him before God. That was given by grace—by the sacrifice of Jesus Christ. Grace is something we all need, but we cannot earn it or give it to others. It comes only through the sacrifice of Christ. Mercy, though, is something we need at various points in our lives and is something we are expected to show toward others. Notice these words from Christ, given in the message we know as the Sermon on the Mount: *"Blessed are the merciful, for they shall obtain mercy"* (Matthew 5:7). We have all gone through times in our lives when we have been in need of mercy. How much mercy are we showing? Grace includes the unmerited gift of salvation and many other expressions of God's grace and with these gifts comes responsibilities and expectations from our Creator. God is faithful and just to forgive us and show unmerited favor. I have seen so many around me who have been shown grace and favor from the Lord even when they did not deserve it. God does not treat us as our sins deserve. We go throughout our daily lives thinking that we can make it in this world without God and if it wasn't for God's grace and mercy a lot of us could have been dead and gone. God is longsuffering and He is trying to give us enough time to make it right with Him. He wants all of His children to be saved. We have been set free from bondage when Jesus died on the cross for our sins. I sit and wonder where I would be if God had not shown me grace and mercy. There were times where I cried myself to sleep wondering how God was going to get me out of a troubling situation and how long it would take for Him to do it. I thank God daily for His grace and mercy that has kept and brought me this far. I don't believe that God has brought me this far to leave me either. Everything I have learned was through God's grace that has taught me patience. It has never been a moment where I was facing adversity and God did not show me mercy and grace. I can go on and on how God will show you grace and mercy in your times of trouble, but you have to receive it. When God frees you from something, don't go back to where and what He freed you from!

Because, when we go back to what God freed us from, the situation will only get worse. God's grace is sufficient and His mercy endureth forever!

CHAPTER 6

DELIVERANCE TESTIMONIES

This Chapter is designed to give insight and share real life deliverance testimonies. There is a no *TESTIMONY* without a *TEST* and no *MESSAGE* without a *MESS*. I know everyone has a story to tell. In life, there are troubling situations that we face that will shake our lives upside down, and the only way we can be delivered from them is with the help of God. God can DELIVER!!! He will turn your situation around but you have to make the first step so God can do the rest. These **deliverance testimonies** are from people that have been set free, healed, and restored! Their stories are phenomenal and will inspire you. Here are some REAL testimonies from others that I got permission to share that may help you or someone in the process of your deliverance:

Jesus Christ saved me from paranoia schizophrenia and blessed me with my degree

When I was in my first year of University (2011), I began having difficulty with my thinking and getting blanks while thinking. I eventually failed my first year. The next year I began a new degree program BSc Chemistry but due to what had happened the previous year, I lost confidence in myself and my identity of being a "smart girl", I decided to hang out with the wrong crowd. I had always been a bit introverted so my transition into a party animal had its dire consequences. I became paranoid and thought that people had snuck a camera into my room. I couldn't focus much on my studies and began overdosing on Ritalin to try and catch up on work and so that I was never myself in front of "the camera". I later began hearing voices that year as well. I never stopped to question it and continued to believe such until I couldn't take it anymore and moved out to a commune. Surprisingly, I came to the conclusion that there were cameras in my room everywhere and just lost all my self-confidence and sense of control. I wanted to tell my parents that I thought there was a "camera" in my room but I knew that they would say that I was crazy and just making things up in my head due to stress but at that time it all felt so real. I began sleeping with guys and having them sleep over in my room so that I couldn't be the only one on "camera". I spent most of my time in bed. All seemed manageable until my final years of university (2015-2016) , this was when all hell broke loose and I began hearing voices commenting on my actions and talking aloud when I wanted to study (I thought it was an earpiece). I just always cried and cried and felt so alone.

I couldn't tell anyone because I felt stupid and thought people snuck in my room and set it up while I was asleep, to pull a 'cruel prank' on me. I just concluded that even in university years there were still people who acted like teenagers. I thought of suicide multiple times but never did anything because I loved my family. I remember things got so bad I thought that they were Satanists and one time during my sorrow-filled days…I chose to ask an 'unclean spirit' to help me handle the pain and to get back at them. I was so broken and emotionally tortured….I reduced myself to saying that day. The next year, I heard the voices dictating my thoughts in other people's voices as well as the banging of drums. I cried and just picked up the Bible and read and prayed the entire night because I was just so frightened out of my skin. I was terrified! I didn't go to campus and wasn't focusing much on my degree. I began focusing more on the Bible and its verses. I began to read it day in and day out and praying to the Lord Jesus Christ. I prayed that He would save me. My condition grew worse and I began to have intrusive thoughts. I would be busy thinking something when another thought was heard. I was creeped out. Then, finally the day arrived when I was walking on campus and I began to feel a loss of control in my walk. It felt like I wasn't controlling my walk, my facial expressions, or my emotions. Throughout this entire time I was hearing voices. I began feeling weird sensations in my body and I headed home feeling as though my feet weren't mine. I couldn't determine the speed of my walk. I went home and cried and cried and prayed and prayed. As the days went by I regained control of my body. I just prayed and prayed and read the Bible until it became my main focus. It was my first time reading the Bible. Months went by where I stayed in my room. It soon seemed like I was handling everything fine. I went to campus and did my work, but my campus life took a spin when people began bringing up memories of when I was a prostitute. It was confusing for me at this point because I couldn't tell the difference as to whether it was real or I was going crazy again. I would still brave the day with the help of Jesus Christ. The semester ended and I had failed all my modules. I didn't seem to care at that point because I knew that the knowledge I had learnt from the Bible was of far more value than any of the modules I failed. I appealed and came back the following semester and studied but kept my main focus on the Bible. There were a few days that I would break down and begin talking to myself and consider suicide but I pushed through. The following year I was completely fine. I went with my Mom (after telling her everything) to a neurologist who diagnosed my condition at the time as "Psychosis due to depression". I don't care what it was labeled as I just know that Jesus Christ helped me through it and that without Him I would never had gone through my "psychosis" and gotten my Bachelor of Sciences. – *Judith T.*

Jesus delivered me from emptiness

Hi all, I know by the looks of the title, it isn't really a pressing issue for anyone, but seriously it has taken a toll on me at one point, constantly seeking a chatting buddy online. If one did not work out, I would continue to seek for another one or have multiple ones (all males) so that I could have people constantly chatting with me, to fill the void in my heart. This went on for 6 years daily and I didn't think it was an issue back then. You know the more you share with people, the more you develop an emotional bond so I felt that I could not leave these guys/the chatting platform. I was all along a Christian, went to church regularly. One day while attending a church service, BAM, I had a revelation. Jesus told me that I CAN leave this platform. I have choices (you just know it's Him speaking, it was very strongly felt and I was very sure of His voice from attending church regularly). The desire to seek for a chatting partner ceased at that moment.

I KNEW I WAS SET FREE THEN. This is bondage by the devil. This is not the life Jesus has called you to live, He wants you to have a partner (a man of God to do life with you) physically, not someone online to fill the void in your heart. For 6 years I could not stop looking for people to chat with, it was compulsive; it was not something I could stop. But ever since the desire ceased, I have since stopped chatting with anyone online for one year. I didn't feel like I need it anymore. Jesus is the only one that can fill your heart. Don't look for men to fill you emotionally. BONDAGE IS BY THE DEVIL. God is love, He wants to fill you, be set free. Before this, I proclaimed I am the righteousness of God in Christ every time I felt prompted to. So proclaim that you are the righteousness of God in Christ, you are right with Him, you don't have to earn this righteousness. It's a gift. Feel empty no more. God will never leave you nor forsake you. Throughout the times I felt empty inside, now I realize that I wasn't empty. I am whole inside. God has always been there for me. As I rested upon God's word, I knew then that I was complete. Amen.-*Rachel M.*

God brought me out of my Depression

I used to be extremely depressed. This depression was without a cause and I was only sad because I had recently begun to know of Emo and Goth culture. It appealed to me, and for a while I became a negative Nancy, blowing little things out of proportion and basically making things seem way worse than they really were. I wanted to be able to act like I was edgy and I wanted to make it seem like I had gone through horrible things. I wasn't delighting in the Lord and was sad all the time and I wasn't that close to Him either. Then, came summer. About 2 weeks after my 8th grade graduation, one night, me and my family were about to play cards. I was just doing my business, getting ready to get called to play them, and then suddenly, I felt a strong wave of sadness come over me. I had no idea what it was, since I had never truly felt sad before. I hadn't experienced true depression until that moment. So, when it came, I had no idea how to counter it or fight it. My family kept asking what was wrong because I had declined playing cards with them. Since I didn't know what was wrong, I couldn't explain what was happening to me. I just said that I started feeling bad. I went to bed hoping, and I think praying, that whatever had come over me would be gone the next day. When I awoke, I found that it didn't. Practically the whole summer, I think I cried every single day. I didn't know what was wrong with me. Along with my depression, I was also tempted to do all sorts of sinful and despicable things. I got closer to

Deliverance, Is My testimony

God through all of that and started reading my Bible more. If it wasn't for Him, well, I don't want to think of where I'd be. So through my bouts of sadness and emotional moments, with Him, I stayed hopeful and never gave up faith. I knew that what was happening to me was a trial and didn't come upon me without reason. I watched Christian movies and listened to Gospel for most of those days. By the end of summer, I began to feel better, not 100%, but I knew that I was getting better and better by the day with the help of God on my side. I realized that God has always been there. High school began, and though I had a rough start with God, I managed to get through and survive my first two years. Then, came year 11. Over the summer, before my 11th grade year of school, the depression came back and it was worse than the first time because this time it came on stronger. I started my 11th grade year feeling slightly better and I did fine the first 2 months, but by the end of October, I noticed I started to forget things. It was becoming harder for me to write and remember things. Stuff I had no difficulty doing gradually became harder. And I started having trouble sleeping. It was only after a few weeks that I came upon the realization that I had been getting no sleep at all. I hadn't noticed because I had never had insomnia before. So because of my lack of sleep,

Deliverance, Is My testimony

I started forgetting how to write full 5 paragraph essays, write full open ended responses and other things. I started to think that I might forget my own name! The enemy kept putting horrible thoughts in my head constantly. I kept trying not to give in to his lies. The thing I should've done was to take captive every thought that was not of Christ and make every single one obedient to Christ. The whole time I was being tormented by the devil and no matter how hard I tried to sleep, every night I would toss and turn, and lie awake. This was torture for me, and pretty soon, I began to lose weight and not really look like myself anymore. People stared at me a lot, and began to start avoiding me. It hurt and I didn't tell my friends what was going on with me. I walked around feeling like a zombie, wondering why I was still alive. I prayed to God a lot, and read my Bible more. Because of Him I never truly lost hope. It did get so bad though, because I started feeling my pulse a lot because I honestly felt like I was going to die. That whole season was truly torture for me and lasted for a span of about 2 months. But on New Year's Day, since my family knew I was struggling so hard, at about12 AM, I think my mother told me and my brother to come into her room. There, we prayed prayers for the New Year, and other things. That night, I lay down to sleep, not expecting to get rest at all. I didn't think I would ever be able to peacefully sleep ever again. But for the first time in about 2 months, I laid down, and I rested, and finally dreamed again. When I awoke, I wasn't sure if I had slept or not. Several months later, I realized that that I did sleep that night and because I hadn't rested in so long, I didn't realize it at the time. After that, I continued to sleep and to dream and God restored me. I got my memory back, I was able to write full essays again, not be anxious about tests anymore and etc. I got closer to God after that and I thank Him for all that I went through because it turned out to be very worth it. So, then near the end of my senior year, I started having trouble staying asleep. I asked God something close to, *"Please don't let this be as bad as it was last time. Lord please make this more bearable for me."* He answered my prayers. I didn't get any sleep, but I started getting 6 hours of sleep a night and then I think I began to only have 3-4 hours of sleep a night. But I got sleep every single night. I became sluggish and a bit anxious and etc. but God helped me through that time. I read the Bible and through this whole thing, I learned how to meditate on God's word. This was something, I didn't really know how to do before, but once I learned how to do it, I kept doing it and it gave me a sense of peace. Also now, with God's help, this time I began to look up ways on how to cure insomnia, and most of the tips worked for me. I survived that season by the grace of God. During the summer of my first semester of college, I started to get closer to God. I started to stop listening to music with sinful explicit lyrics; I stopped lusting after boys, etc. I really was trying to just get closer to Him. I talked to Him more, and I noticed that the more I talked to Him, the more the enemy tried to come into my mind. I kept asking the Lord to deliver me from the evil thoughts that kept coming into my mind and into my head popped the verse: *"But he said to me, "My grace is sufficient for you, for my power is made perfect in weakness." Therefore I will boast all the more gladly about my weaknesses, so that Christ's power may rest on me."*(2 Corinthians 12:19). The thoughts kept coming on more and more and became more intrusive and blasphemous. One night, it got so bad that I began to pray so fervently to the Lord. I asked Him to strengthen me and I prayed for others and for all the other believers in the world. I promised Him that I would get closer to Him and that I would do what I needed to do to do so. The next day, after I had rested, I awoke and the thoughts started to come into my head. I took them all captive repeatedly, and the Lord filled my head with lots of encouraging verses. I kept notes of all of them, and began to say some them out loud whenever He reminded me of one. He granted me His peace and I could feel that He was strengthening me. He didn't leave me at all and He heard me when I cried out to Him. So, I want any of you to declare the word over your life. Remember that you are more than conquerors through Him who loved you (Romans 8:37) and that that no weapon formed against you will prosper (Isaiah 54:17). Always count it all joy that you endure trials (James 1:2-3). Always put on the armor of God and never take it off (Ephesians 6:10-18) and remember to never be anxious but make all your prayers and requests be made known to God. Then, you will receive His peace. (Philippians 4:6-7). And never forget to rebuke the devil and any other evil spirits in Christ Jesus and take captive every single thought and make them obedient to Christ (2 Corinthians 10:5).We believers never suffer without reason because we know that our trials will help us to persevere more.(James 1:12). Whatever has happened to you will work out for good for those who love God (Romans 8:28) so ask God to grant you His peace and to give you the strength to help you endure whatever you're going through. With faith, believe that He will bring you out of whatever ordeal has come upon you. God loves you and He would never have you to go through anything without it making you better. I've learned that God will put no more on me than I could bear. I kept the faith!-*Lynette C.*

Overcoming a Porn Addiction

I'm writing this to share my personal experience with pornography. Jesus says to the Samaritan woman in John 4:13-14 says, *"Everyone who drinks of this water will be thirsty again, but whoever drinks of the water that I will give him will never be thirsty again."* Pornography was the substance I constantly consumed and needed more of each time. It was an idol available to me at all times where I could go to when I was stressed out or just needed a boost in my day. I had no way of knowing that it would turn my world upside down. For my whole existence I have struggled with searching for satisfaction in my life. I looked to drugs, alcohol, and lawlessness to fill this. All of these seemed to have detrimental effects on my life except for pornography. I was first exposed to pornographic material while I was in elementary school. I remember coming across a few Playboy magazines and saw hundreds of beautiful women with bodies that seemed out of this world. This encounter shaped how I would view females for the next decade of my life. I was constantly seeking porn online during my free time and fantasizing about it during the day. Sex was on my mind 24/7. My life was changed the summer after freshman year of college. My porn habit had escalated to an area of no return. I had downloaded every hookup app and was even starting to search on craigslist, meeting random women to fuel my hunger for sexual promiscuity. I had been engaging in sexual activities via webcam as well and I was viewing the most explicit pornography content available. I knew this was very destructive and tried countless times to stop, but this addiction had taken over my life. *Be sure your sin will find you out-* Numbers 32:23. I was participating in an "inappropriate" activity online with a person I thought was a woman that I had met online. I soon came to realize after a few minutes that this person was not whom they said they were. This person had recorded what I was doing, and played it back to me so I could see it. They threatened to upload that video online and send it to everyone I knew unless I sent them $500. I was so embarrassed and quickly went to get my wallet but soon realized, what would stop them from coming back and demanding more money? At that point, I immediately knew I was trapped. I sat in the darkness of my room, reflecting on my life and how every action I had sowed led me to this moment. I thought about how this would be the last day of my life, and how this addiction had dictated the way I had lived for most of my life. I had never believed in a God, but in that moment I just so badly needed a higher being to watch over and protect me. I said countless prayers to a God that I hoped was listening to save me from ending my life and that I would dedicate the rest of my life to Him if He could get me out of that dark place. I now know that's really not how Christianity works but I knew that I needed help to turn my life around. Fast forward a month later; I never heard from the person again and I ended up joining a wonderful Christian organization at my school called Intervarsity. For so much of my life, I felt so sorry for Christians. I always thought about how terrible it is to worship a God who limits you in so many areas of your life and tells you stuff you're not allowed to do. I was so wrong. God sets us free from the chains that we are bound to and releases us from being slaves to the wicked masters that we are serving. I found ways to conquer your porn addiction: Acknowledgement – Confess your addiction to the Lord. *"He who conceals his transgressions will not prosper, but he who confesses and forsakes them will find compassion."* – Proverbs 28:13. Social Circle- Have a few good friends who you can talk to about your struggles with porn and who will encourage you to destroy this addiction. It'll be so much tougher to overcome your addiction if you only have friends who watch and joke about their porn habit. *"Bad company corrupts good character"* (1 Corinthians 15:33). Constantly surround yourself with people – It is nearly impossible to watch porn with other people around. The biggest temptations to watch porn arise when you're in your room by yourself. Find some fun activities to do with friends. *"It is not good for man to be alone"* (Genesis 2:18) Study the word of God- God doesn't hate sex; He loves it! He is the one who created it after all. God hates seeing the abuse of sex. Sex is meant to be under the confines of a marriage and is the act of two people joining together as one flesh under God.-*John B.*

<u>*Rescued from the Deepest Pits*</u>

I will begin my testimony from childhood. I remember at the age of five, I was living with my father. My mother was never around because she was sentenced to life in prison for murdering her husband and her father. She was drug addicted, mentally ill, and a victim of abuse her whole life. Well, I was living with my dad who sold methamphetamine and crack cocaine and did it daily. He was never around; he was always out partying and selling drugs. I was left home with his girlfriends. When I was six, I began huffing gasoline and spray paint fumes to escape my sadness and confusion. I would have hallucinations of funny voices that would make me laugh and feel happy, and I would see things as well. After a while, it took a dark tone and the voices would torment me and put me down and make things worse. I felt so alone. I was always in the woods as a child, alone and secluded in nature. Finally, I got placed in foster care for like a year. During that time, I was bullied and locked in dark closets and I don't remember much else. My father got me back and I was 8. From 8 until 10, I lived with him. He was still distant. I remember one day he smacked me on the head and it hurt and I was so fed up, I went in this back yard behind some house and crawled in an old, dirty doghouse. I never prayed in my life or knew anything about God, but I begged God to take me from my dad that day. When I went into foster care at age 10, the first place I went was a shelter for bad children due to the foster homes being full. I was sexually assaulted my first night by a 16 year old. The first foster home I went to after that was with a woman who was a witch and it was terrible there. In the next two years, I was placed in over 20 foster homes. I went to over 10 elementary schools and two middle schools. I couldn't make friends because I knew I would soon be shipped to another home. I stopped unpacking my trash bag of clothes when I arrived at new homes as well. Everyone I tried to ever attach to get taken from me, so I cut my emotions off and walked around numb and isolated and didn't open up or attach to anyone. 8 months before I turned 12, I moved with an older lady that basically forced me to go to church every Wednesday and Sunday. These services lasted 3+ hours and the churches were small and hot with no air conditioner and I live in Florida. I couldn't stand church. Over the next month, I grew fond of it. One Wednesday night at service, they did altar call to get saved. I began crying hysterically and felt a burning desire to go up there and I have no thought or hesitation, I simply walked up there and got saved. It was the best day of my life. Six months later I got adopted by a wealthy, loving family. They adopted me at 12 and I lived with them until I was 14. After I got adopted, I slowly stopped praying all the time like I had been since I was saved, I put God on the back burner and felt I didn't need Him. During my time with them, not having a mother or father or stable friendship with anyone my whole life made me fear love. Every time I ever loved, I was hurt, and my adopted parents loved me so much and it terrified me. I was diagnosed with borderline personality disorder and was on medication since I was 11, and an SSI check. I was so afraid of abandonment that I put them through so much so they would have to prove they would never leave me. They had to show me they were committed to me. I got suspended from school, I got 27 referrals in a school year, I was skipping class, skipping school, not doing chores at home, and staying in my room constantly to avoid the family. I put a strain on their marriage and they divorced. At 14, they placed me back in foster care where I caught 7 charges within a months' time. I began smoking marijuana and synthetic drugs as well. I was incarcerated from age 15 to age 17. It was a youth prison and I began cutting myself in there. I also began fighting and praying to Satan. It never occurred to me that I had given up on God. I always thought He gave up on me. I got out and got back in public school with my adopted mom and began smoking weed again and cutting myself daily with razor blades. I was committed to a psychiatric hospital 4 times and stayed from a week to 2 months each time. I was practicing Satanism with some kid at my school as well. I began becoming obsessed with Satan and demons. Finally, a week before my 18th birthday, my real dad found me on Facebook, messaged me, and invited me to come meet him. I told him I'd like to move in because I never stopped loving my dad and didn't realize he never changed. My adopted mom took me there to live with him. After one day, he kicked me out. My adopted mom wouldn't let me come back with her either so I swallowed a bottle of my sleeping pills and slept for like 4 days and woke up in a psychiatric hospital. When I was released from there, I lived with my dad's old friend from my childhood. Also, he was now married to my stepmom who raised me when my dad was gone selling drugs. She was a witch and her mom who owned the house and lived with them was a witch as well, she did rituals all the time. He sold drugs and he gave me drugs all the time so I dropped out of school at 18 so I could sit home and get high all day. I lived there six months and he kicked me out on and off because he was on every drug pretty much and he had mood swings. I was still cutting myself through this time. Pretty much from that point at 18 through the next 5 years, I kept cutting myself, got 8 charges, spent over a year in the county jail, got admitted to psychiatric hospitals over 20 times, wasn't on my medication, was in and out of the streets, tried committing suicide 4 times, cooking methamphetamine, began using drugs through a needle, stealing from stores habitually, having sex with a lot of women, stealing cars, breaking in homes, was in and out of rehab 5 times as well. I stopped practicing Satanism due to my life falling apart, and at 20. I started practicing new age spirituality. It's on YouTube called spirit science. Also at this time, I began huffing gasoline again since my youth and using psychedelic drugs as well to hallucinate. I was meditating, trying to astral project, lucid dreaming, calling out to "spirit guides", getting into crystals, Ouija boards. Bad stuff. But it seemed nice, I was blinded. I opened my third eye "chakra" and began hearing voices. They were soft at first, over time they got louder. They were funny. Hilarious even. They seemed to relate to me on a deep level, then, over time, they started suggesting I kill people, kill myself, cut myself, and pray to Satan. That's when I realized it was demonic. That's when I also realized that at age six on up through foster care, those groups of voices sitting around me were demons. When I was high on synthetic drugs and felt three presences in the room with me and had conversations with them, they were demons. I started séance rituals at six years old but had no clue they were real things. I asked its name when I realized it was demonic and it took a few minutes but it said "Abaddon" I googled it to see if it was real or not or just my imagination. Sure enough, the name is in revelations. A demon to be released from the pits of hell in the end times. That's when I turned back to Christ and praying again. Well, I kept getting high. Drug addiction had me in its vice grip. Just as it had my mother, my dad, my aunt, my uncle, and my two other uncles who are dead as a result of it now. So, I kept doing these hallucinogens and one day I heard a voice that wasn't demonic say that I was going to a mental institution, and that would lose my girlfriend that I had been with for two years, and I would be locked away for six months. It was a still voice. All these things took place in the next six months because I overdosed again. When I got out of the mental hospital, I wanted to hear about my future again so I did drugs and asked to know what was in store for my future. I was told this girl I was getting high with that I just met for the first time would be kicked out of her house; we would get in a relationship. I saw a vision of us lying in the grass, and then I was told we would go through a dark period. It all happened in the month. Some things that were shown to me did not happen though. The dark period we went through was 6 months in jail for grand theft from Wal-Mart. I got out and I was close to God from being in jail. I still wanted to look into the future though so I tried and it wasn't really working, so I kept trying. It wasn't working. One night I was so depressed. You see, the mental disorder I have makes me have mood swings that switch so quickly. One time, I was suicidal depressed and literally eight minutes later, I was joyful. Nothing triggers it. It is random. But it's up to 20+ times in a single day and this night I was fed up and I had a bottle of pills I knew would be lethal if I took. I was about to take them when I prayed to God. I said please show me if I have a purpose on this earth. Give me a reason to live or I'm taking my life right now. He showed me going to a drug rehab program, getting a license and car, getting back with my ex-girlfriend, going to college for animation and art, getting out of college and working for Pixar animating Disney movies. He showed me and my ex-girlfriend being married and I saw both of our children and the house we would have and I saw great wealth. So much money. But I was so filled with the Holy Spirit; I was weeping and so grateful. This was the first time a vision was from God and not demons since the first time it happened. This felt calmer, more still, and put me in so much peace, and it was a trance. I told God I don't want to work for the world; I want to work for you. I was so grateful to Him I wanted to give Him my life. He then showed me quitting Pixar after a few years, buying my own animation studio, animating the Bible for children and it being put on YouTube and translated in many languages and sent to many countries to touch the next generation. I'm trying not to cry typing this, it's such a blessing. Then selling the rights to my animated movie and getting a TON of money for it. By that point it will be time for me to build my own church and become a pastor. It makes sense; I never believed it until He showed me. My ex-girlfriend used to dream that I was a pastor, when I got baptized in rehab. She stated, a woman said God showed her a vision of me preaching to a gigantic church. One pastor at this Christian rehab said when everyone prayed over me, he felt I was greatly anointed, and this woman who sees visions from God told me when she saw me in church for the first time, she felt in her spirit that God has huge plans for me. I'm so blessed and humble. One time when I was high a voice even said 'since you love God maybe you should be a pastor.' I just laughed it off and never thought about it. I doubted God's ability to use such a dirty sinner for His glory. The thing is though, in the Bible, Jesus devoted His time and energy, teaching mainly to the worst sinners. Look at Paul for example, my middle name is Paul which I find ironic, but a Christian therapist once told me the deeper the pit you allow God to pull you out of, the higher rank you will have in His army. Since then, when I used hallucinogenic drugs, it wasn't enjoyable anymore. I was attacked, threatened, screamed at, hated, and it just was traumatic. These demons came after me so hard since then. They bribe me, showing me living in a mansion with exotic cars and women and waterfalls and swimming pools.

Deliverance, Is My testimony

They say they will give me anything I could want on this earth. Anything I ask for. They want my soul, they say it straight up. They want it badly, but I would never turn back to that wickedness. They would say I'm a high value target and they have a target on my back. I don't fear though, the blood of Jesus got me through all I have been through, and if you are a saved Christian, in the spiritual realm, you have a wall of fire surrounding you, and demons can't touch you. No demon no matter how powerful can come against the blood of Jesus Christ. They tremble at His name. Well, a Minister at this Christian rehab I was at told me I have the gift of prophecy. I have dreams seeing visions of things that always happen the next day. I was using demons to practice sorcery to look into the future, but since I chose to give my life to God, He used that for His glory. I go to rehab in three months and I'm working on getting as close to the Lord as I can. This rehab will be the one where I turn my life around through Him. He showed me this being the right time in that vision two years ago. So I have much growing to go, but I felt like I should go ahead and put this out there. Thank you for listening.-*Shawn V.* Listen, sometimes being able to share your deliverance testimony takes courage. I have conquered my own demons and have been able to overcome troubling situations with the help of God. I am still waiting for deliverance from something that I have been praying about for quite some time now. God's timing is perfect and in the process while you're waiting to be delivered, you need strength from God to remain strong. God takes care of His own. I've learned that you have to want to make a change in your life. With these powerful testimonies, God has turned their darkest days into light to use their tragic situations for His glory. The miracle of salvation is free! Christian testimonies can have a very powerful effect upon those in desperate need of encouragement. Are you a Christian who has received forgiveness and perhaps miracles and deliverance through Jesus, and what He did on the cross? Perhaps you can tell about your conversion experience, or how He brought you through difficult times. You may have been delivered from some tragedy by the power of God, or experienced a wonderful miracle. Now you can share what God has done for you. "*And they overcame him by the blood of the Lamb and by the word of their testimony...*" (Revelation 12:11). A well-shared testimony can paint a powerful WORD PICTURE in the mind of the hearer or reader. People remember word pictures much longer than just stated facts. Jesus told parables because they form powerful *word pictures* in our mind, as well as convey a spiritual message/s. A well-shared testimony can do the same thing. How can you share your testimony with others? **BEFORE**: Give details of your life *before* you became serious about having a personal relationship with Jesus Christ. What type of environment were you raised in? What were your beliefs about God? What were your *struggles* with God? What were your beliefs about the Bible? What did the death, burial, and resurrection of Jesus Christ on the cross mean to you? What was your understanding of this incredible sacrifice for your sins? **DURING:** Your number one purpose for testifying is to give Jesus Christ glory (heart-felt thanks and showing appreciation) for what He has done in your life *and* to advance the Kingdom of God (help win souls to Jesus Christ). In so doing, you honor and glorify the Father as well as the Holy Spirit. Describe the circumstances in detail that caused you to get serious about turning your life over to Jesus Christ. Most people's actions spring out of their unsatisfied, deep inner needs. What were the unsatisfied, deeps inner need(s) that you had that the Holy Spirit used to draw you to a personal relationship with Jesus Christ? *Here are some examples of deep, inner needs: Lack of peace. Fear of death/hell. Something missing-void in your life. No meaning to life. Loneliness. Lack of security. Poverty. Lack of purpose. Longing to be loved.*

Deliverance, Is My testimony

Longing to be unconditionally accepted. No real friends. No motivation. Alcohol or chemical dependencies. Eating disorders. Guilt from sin - needing forgiveness. Hopelessness-prison. Boredom with religion. Demonic activity in your life. Need of deliverance-healing. Hunger to know God better. Feelings that God betrayed you. **<u>AFTER</u>:** Share how your relationship with Jesus Christ has changed you. Why are you excited about your relationship with Christ *now?* Give the details! As you write your testimony ... is sensitive to the Holy Spirit about interweaving scripture into your testimony. Use a Bible translation that is easy to understand. Remember -- God promises that His Word will "not come back to Him void" (See: Isaiah 55:11). It is usually better to write a testimony that you think is too long rather than one that is too brief, when submitting it for publication. A long testimony can always be shortened, but too brief of a testimony cannot be made longer by an editing staff. Take time to share miraculous events that have happened *after* you got saved, as well as before you got saved. <u>Dynamic answers to prayer</u>, for instance, are so encouraging to other believers. These are very valuable in adding impact to your overall born again testimony. The most effective testimony in reaching the unsaved is *not* sharing a list of *your* "spiritual accomplishments." People searching for spiritual answers want to know how God became *real* and *alive* in your life, and the **positive changes** that God has done in your life. Sharing painful trials you have gone through and how God brought you through them and what you learned through those trials can add an additional anointing of God on your testimony. Never underestimate the value of sharing your trials and how they have strengthened and enriched your relationship with God. Try to use words that the unsaved comprehend the easiest. Stay away from using "religious" words as best as you can. Being transparent – being real – being humble and appreciative and thankful gives God the very best *quality* testimony you could possibly give Him to touch the lives of others. Share your testimony with **passion.** Share it in humility, yet with **excitement!** (No one likes a boring, monotone speaker or writer). Are you in love with God? Tell the world about your love affair with Him! He absolutely delights in seeing you tell others of how much He means to you -- and what He has done for you! "Go tell the world every way you can … what the Lord has done for *you!*" Don't put off sharing (writing especially) your testimony. You don't have tomorrow promised to you ... on this side of eternity anyway!

<u>CONCLUSION</u>

While believers are delivered once and for all time from eternal punishment, we are also delivered from the trials of this life. Sometimes, that deliverance is God simply walking through the trials by our side, comforting and encouraging us through them as He uses them to mature us in faith. Paul assured the Corinthian believers that "no hath temptation has seized you except what is common to man. And, God is faithful. He will not let you be tempted beyond what you can bear. But when you are tempted, He will also provide a way out so that you can stand up under it" (I Corinthians 10:13). In these cases, rescue is not immediate, but in due time, after patience has had its perfect work (James 1:2-4, 12). God makes the way of escape simultaneously in His perfect will and timing. Deliverance is often sought from evil spirits or the spirit of lust, jealousy, envious etc. It's important to understand that as believers, we already have the eternal victory over Satan and demons. But we can be delivered from their influence in our lives by using two weapons God has given us as part of our spiritual armor with which we battle "against the spiritual forces of evil in the heavenly realms" (Ephesians 6:12-17). The believer defends himself with the shield of faith and uses the offensive weapon of the Word of God. I've learned that in order for God to move in your life, you have to want to make a change. You're waiting on God, but He is waiting on you. God is no respector of persons; He treats and loves us all the same. God is always the subject and His people are always the object of deliverance. When you cannot help yourself anymore and no human being can deliver you, when all your ways are fenced in and you see no hope, there is still God. God is always right there by your side. God allows us to go through troubling situations and delivers us out of them so we can help someone else. We can't even comprehend the things God has in store for us. Sometimes when we see things for what they are, we get discouraged. But when we look at it through faith in God's word, we can see things the way God sees it. We may not be able to physically see it but we can spiritually visualize it through faith. When your sins accuse you and you see the need of the Lord Jesus in your heart, trust in Him. Call upon Him with expectation. He will not refuse you. You may lean on the Lord and put your hope in Him. Those who call upon the name of the Lord shall be saved. In spite of all their impossibilities, the Lord can give a full deliverance. Those who wait upon the Lord shall not be put to shame. In our daily lives, the Lord may lead us into impossible situations to show us

Deliverance, Is My testimony

His great power to deliver from every need. The way to receive this deliverance is by prayer. The Lord Jesus has taught us in the parable of the unjust judge and the importunate widow that we should pray continually and we should not give up. At times, the Lord withholds the fulfilment for a while. In His wisdom, He does not always answer immediately. But deliverance comes at exactly the right time. It never comes too soon or too early. The Lord can bear with us for long and can seem to wait a long time before giving full deliverance to His people (Luke 18:7). Whether you are still waiting to be delivered, stay in the faith and let God perform His perfect work in you. God's timing is perfect! Learning to wait on God has taught me patience and being able to endure has given me wisdom. I know what you are going through may seem insurmountable and you may feel like there is no way out. Remember, that God has purpose for your pain and what you are going through is just a setup to be a blessing for someone else. God will not allow for you to go through something that will not be beneficial in the end. Trust God for your deliverance and allow Him to reign in you so that you can be taken to a higher plane. Everyone has a story to tell, so let God use you for His glory to help someone else through their deliverance. God sees everything from up there and He knows the pain that we are facing while waiting to be delivered. Ask God to keep you strong throughout the process and don't let your wait for God be in vain. When Jesus died on the cross, we were set free. Don't continue to live in bondage and under the lies of Satan because he will keep you stagnated if you let him. Say YES to be delivered today!!!

BIOGRAPHY OF THE AUTHOR

Lucretia Shaw Cargill is a wife and mother of two beautiful daughters who is on a mission to empower, encourage, inspire, and uplift all individuals who are seeking and desiring a way to ultimately know how to start walking in a different direction to get a different result in life. Native of Selma, Alabama. Lucretia is an Author/Publisher, Inspirational Speaker, Radio Host and Podcaster who is on a mission to make an IMPACT in the world. Since the course of her writing, she is now a Christian Blogger and provides Self-Publishing and Ghostwriting services. Lucretia is on a mission to change the lives of those around her. Founder of Women's Empowerment Group called the "*DIVINE TRUTH*" to encourage, empower, and uplift women daily. Lucretia strives for perfection to reach her goals and success to seize every opportunity to help both men and women to overcome any challenges they face in life that may be hindering and blocking them from receiving the blessings that God has laid and stored up for them. From understanding God's purpose and plan for her life, her advice and insight will help countless individuals who want to activate and take control of their lives. Lucretia empowers thousands of people to take charge of the difficult situations that may be standing in their way and things that may have an impact of changes daily. Lucretia is very compassionate towards her readers and is dedicated and devoted to keep it real in all circumstances. Lucretia's straightforwardness and genuine lifestyle will attract different social organizations and institutions that are ready to handle the TRUTH!!

<u>NOTES</u>

Made in the
USA
Columbia, SC